The essential knot book

The essential knot book

THE SEAMANSHIP SERIES

Colin Jarman

drawings by Bill Beavis

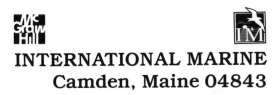

INTERNATIONAL MARINE
Camden, Maine 04843

Published by International Marine®

20 19 18 17 16 15 14 13 12 11

Library of Congress Cataloging-in-Publication Data

Jarman, Colin
  The essential knot book.

  (The Seamanship series)
  Includes index.
  1. Knots and splices. I. Title II. Series
VM5333.J36 1986   623.88'82   86-2775
ISBN 0-87742-221-4

Questions regarding the content of this book should be
addressed to:

International Marine
P.O. Box 220
Camden, ME 04843

Printed by BookCrafters, Inc., Chelsea, Michigan

Acknowledgement
The author wishes to thank both Marlow Ropes Ltd and
Bridon Fibres and Plastics Ltd for their help during the
production of this book.

Contents

Some rope terms explained

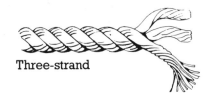

Three-strand

Multiplait

Sixteen-plait with three-strand core

Braided with braided core

Bight. The middle of a line or, more commonly, a curve or loop taken in a line well away from either end.

Bitter end. The end of a line, rope or wire.

Core. Centre of rope. Modern ropes have separately constructed core and covering (sheath).

Core strand (heart strand). Straight strand running through centre (core, heart) of wire rope.

Fall. End of halyard that is handled, winched and cleated.

Fibres. Smallest part of rope made collectively into yarns which are in turn made up into strands that are then used to form the whole rope.

Frapping turns. Turns of rope binding things together.

Heart strand (core strand). Straight strand running through centre of wire rope.

Lay. The 'twist' pattern of a three strand rope.

Lay up. Twist strands together to form a rope.

Marry. Interweave unlayed strands prior to splicing together.

Milk. The sheath of a rope is slipped down over a splice by 'milking' it.

Round turn. A rope's end makes a round turn on something when it passes right around it through 540 degrees to enclose the object and point back parallel to its own standing part.

Serve. Cover over either with tight binding of light twine or, more commonly nowadays, adhesive tape.

Sheath. The outside cover of a plaited 'core and sheath' rope.

Standing part. The main, non-working part of a line.

Stop, to. To lash, seize or tape over temporarily, usually to prevent unlaying.

Strand. Constituent part of rope. First subdivision, eg three strand laid rope.

Thimble. Plastic or metal shaped eye inserted into spliced eye.

Throat. Point at which two parts of rope re-unite after passing round thimble or forming soft eye.

Tuck, to. Weave ends of strands into laid up rope to make splice.

Unlay, to. Open up and separate strands of laid rope or unravel plaited rope.

Whip, to. Bind rope's end to prevent unlaying.

Whipping. Binding on rope's end preventing unlaying.

Worm. Spiral along groove between strands of laid rope.

Yarns. Fibres are twisted together to form yarns, which are in turn used to make up strands forming rope.

Standing
part

Bitter
End

Bight

Turn

Round turn

1 Knots, bends and hitches

Reef Knot

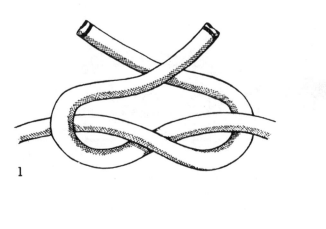

1

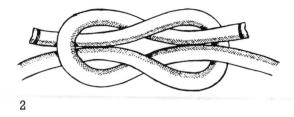

2

Originally used to tie off the ends of reef points when shortening sail, this symmetrical, flat knot can be formed with load on both standing parts and can also be untied under tension by pulling on one end and capsizing the knot. It is unsuitable for joining ropes together, but if used to do so, the ropes must be of equal size and type otherwise it will slip.

A Reef Knot is formed with two overhand knots tied in opposite directions so that ends lie back alongside standing parts on their same sides.

A Reef Knot fastening a gasket round a furled sail.

A Reef Knot securing an anchor to its deck chocks.

Slipped Reef Knot

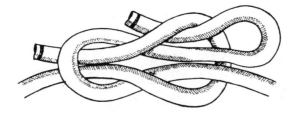

Formed in just the same way as a Reef Knot, but with one end doubled through to look like half a bow (look at your shoe laces). The advantage comes when trying to undo the knot if it has worked up very tight. The doubled end can then be given a good, hard pull and the first overhand knot falls undone. The load will then release the second part. It's very good if your fingers are cold and numb.

Figure of Eight

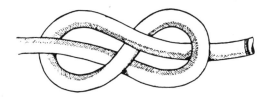

This knot looks just like its name – a number 8. It is a stopper knot formed in the bitter end of a rope to prevent its running out through a block, sheave or fairlead. Thus it is generally used in halyard falls, sheet ends, reefing lines, kicking straps and so on.

It is used in preference to an overhand knot by seamen as it is bulkier, thus preventing the line running out through larger holes, and it does not bind so tightly, making it easier to undo when required.

Figure of Eight used in bitter
end of kicking strap

Bowline

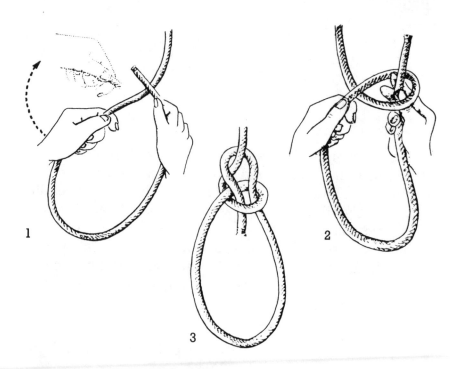

Probably the most useful knot on a boat, the Bowline provides a standing loop in the end of a line. Easy to tie, the knot is also easy to undo even after being under severe load.

There are many ways to tie a Bowline and the end can lie inside or outside the final loop. The easiest way in light line is to apply the end of the line to the standing part, and twist as shown so that it appears through a loop. Then pass round the standing part and back down through the initial loop. This process is a knack, but easily learned.

The Bowline must be worked up tight, particularly in springy synthetic ropes.

Round Turn and Two Half Hitches

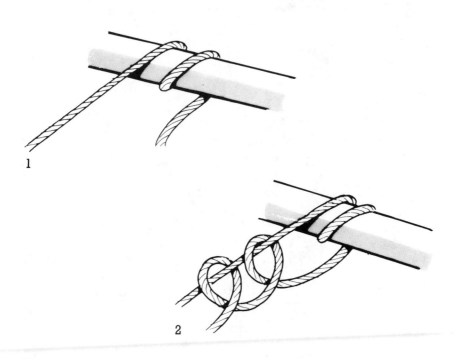

1

2

Usually used to secure a line to a spar, eye or ring, the Hitch is formed by passing the line round the spar (for example) in a complete round turn – so that the spar is completely enclosed by the rope and the bitter end is pointing back down the standing part – then tying what amounts to a Clove Hitch (see page 12) about the standing part. The working end passes round the standing part, crosses itself away from the original Round Turn and goes round again in a second Hitch as can be seen in the photographs.

Common uses include securing fenders to grabrails or guardwires, painters to towing eyes on dinghies or mooring rings on quaysides.

Fisherman's Bend or Anchor Bend

This is very similar in formation to the Round Turn and Two Half Hitches, but is somewhat more secure. As can be seen the working end of the line passes under the Round Turn on the anchor ring so that it is locked under load. The Half Hitches are then put on in the same way as for the Round Turn and Two Half Hitches. Finally the bitter end, for complete security, can either be seized to the standing part as in the photograph or linked to it with a Bowline.

Clove Hitch

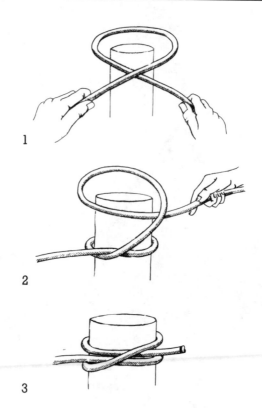

1

2

3

This is a much misused knot. Equal loads (or at least nearly equal) must be applied continuously to both sides otherwise it will roll and eventually undo. Therefore it should *not* be used to moor a boat as all the load will be on one side and the boat will, sooner or later, be lost.

To form the Hitch, the bitter end is either passed round and round the object the line is being hitched to or, if the top is open, preformed loops are dropped over as shown. This method is easier but not always possible. With laid rope, form loops by twisting *with* the lay.

Above: Clove Hitch
used to lash tiller
amidships.
Left: Clove Hitches
used to secure halyard
to burgee stick.

13

Lighterman's Hitch

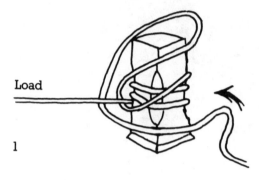

Load

1

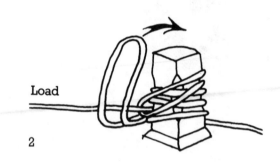

Load

2

This Hitch, also called a Tugboat Hitch and a 'No-name Knot', is particularly useful when taking a tow as it can be released under even the greatest tension. To form, take a round turn on the samson post then pass a bight under the standing part and drop it down over the top of the post. Take another turn (not a round turn) on the post then again pass a bight under the standing part and drop it down over the post. This process can be repeated as often as required to prevent slipping under load.

Sheet Bend
or Becket Bend

Sheet bend

A Sheet Bend is used to join two lines together and is referred to as a Becket Bend when one rope has an eye already spliced in the end.

Where a standing eye does not exist a bight is taken in the end of one line (usually the thicker line) and the end of the other line is passed through it, round the back of the two standing parts and across the eye by threading under itself. The diagram should make this clear, but do take care to finish with the bitter ends of the two lines on the same side. And pull it tight.

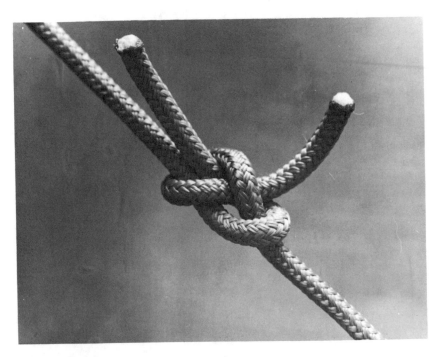

Above: Sheet Bend. Below: Becket Bend.

Double Sheet or Becket Bend

Double sheet bend

For added security a Sheet or Becket Bend (previous page) can quickly be transformed into a Double Bend by taking the working end of line round behind the standing loop and across parallel to itself for a second time.

The Double Bend is inevitably slightly slower to form but is much more secure in slippery or springy synthetic fibre ropes, having far less tendency to fall apart when not under load.

Above: Double Sheet Bend. Below: Double Becket Bend.

Rolling Hitch on Rope

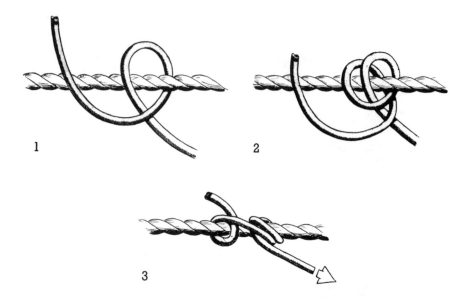

1

2

3

Used to secure one line to another, for example a line being used to relieve tension on another, the Rolling Hitch remains most secure when load is applied from a direction roughly parallel to the standing rope.

The Hitch is formed by taking a turn about the standing rope followed by a second crossing over itself. This immediately locks the line and a final Half Hitch finishes the whole thing off. Greatest security is achieved if the turns are put on *with* the lay of the standing rope.

Occasionally a very stiff or springy synthetic rope will not remain secure when formed into a Rolling Hitch. It slips simply because the turns cannot grip properly. In this case a third initial turn should be taken to help bind the rope to either spar or second rope.

Rolling Hitch
about a Spar

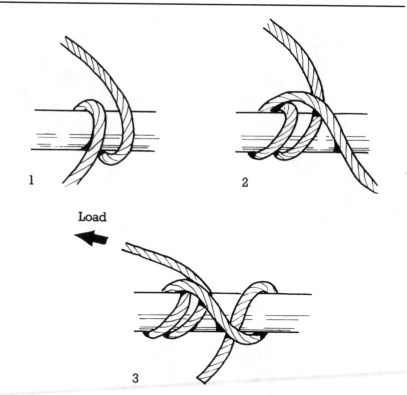

1

2

Load

3

A slightly different form of Rolling Hitch from the basic one described already is used when securing a rope to a spar rather than to another rope. In this case the initial turns do not cross over each other, they simply roll around the spar. The final Half Hitch is still formed beyond the point where the standing part of the line meets the spar.

Figure of Eight Loop

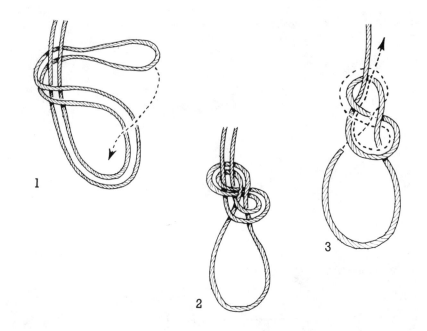

1

2

3

While a Bowline suits almost all purposes where a loop is required, it may not hold in very hard, slippery synthetics and can well be replaced by the Figure of Eight Loop. This is often also used where a loop is required midway along a rope as it is quicker to form than a Bowline on the bight. In this situation a simple Figure of Eight knot is tied with a bight of the rope rather than the bitter end (1 and 2).

Where it has to be tied through an eye or ring, or about an object that a loop cannot be slipped over, the method shown in 3 is used. Tie a Figure of Eight with a long working end and then 'double' it in the reverse direction with the ring or eye enclosed by a suitable loop in the working end. Both processes result in identical knots.

Constrictor Knot

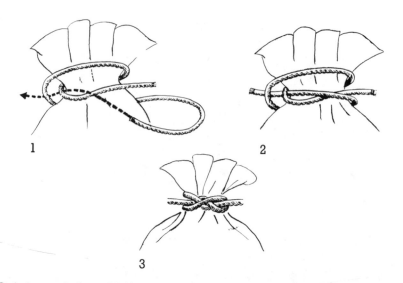

1

2

3

Originated by Clifford W. Ashley, author of the famous *Ashley Book of Knots*, the Constrictor can well be used as a temporary whipping or seizing. It may also serve to tie the neck of a sailbag or kit bag, but in this case a slipped version might be desirable to make eventual undoing easier.

The essence of the knot is that it becomes ever tighter as tension is applied to the ends without loosening as the strain is taken off them.

To form the knot, take a Round Turn with the working end crossing the standing part (like the beginning of a Rolling Hitch) and make an overhand knot beneath the crossover point using the working end and the standing part. This process should be made clear by the diagrams. Then pull as tight as required. For easier untying, form a slipped overhand knot using a bight in the working end.

Surgeon's Knot

This might be described as the Reef Knot for springy or slippery synthetics as it performs the same task but is more secure in modern materials. There are two forms; the more established is formed in the same way as a Reef Knot but with a second turn at each stage. Thus the square knot becomes a rectangle as shown in the diagram.

The second form has two initial overhand knots again, but instead of a second pair on top there is just one. Then, when the knot is drawn up tight the upper overhand knot forms a parallel crossover leaving the ends sticking out on opposite sides. It is not so neat, but when drawn up tightly does form a very secure, locked knot. The photographs show the differences.

Standard Surgeon's Knot.

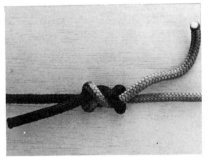

Alternative Surgeon's Knot.

Carrick Bend

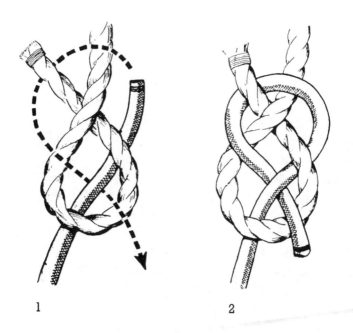

1   2

This is an excellent knot for joining two lines together, whatever their material or relative diameters and is often used for adding an extra line to a kedge warp.

A loop is made in the end of one line with the bitter end crossing the standing part. The working end of the other line is then laid across and underneath the loop, passed over the first line's standing part, under its bitter end, over the first part of the original loop, under itself and over the other side of the original loop. Thus it has been woven alternately over and under each part as shown in the diagrams. When drawn tight the knot capsizes leaving the bitter ends together and parallel.

(Note: The drawings on page 28 show the best configuration.)

29

Sheepshank

Commonly described as a knot for shortening a line temporarily, the Sheepshank has more practical value as a means of bypassing a chafed section of rope.

Where this is the intention, a bight is taken in the line well to one side of the damaged area and brought back alongside the standing part on the other side of the damage. There it is applied to the standing part and twisted, as in the Bowline or Waggoner's Hitch, to leave the bight protruding through a loop in the standing part. The remaining bight is applied to the standing part next to it in the same way. The result is a Sheepshank as shown with the chafed rope in the middle. If formed correctly this can actually be cut through without the knot falling apart so long as tension is maintained. To prevent the Sheepshank falling apart when not under load, seize the 'ears' to the standing parts as shown.

Marling Hitch

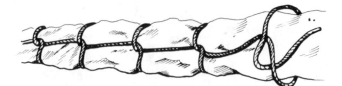

A series of Marling Hitches can be used to lash a sail to its boom or yard or to secure a bundle of sail to a guardrail or to the boom.

Each of the series of Hitches is formed by passing the line down around the sail bundle (for example), up over the part lying along the sail and then tucked down under itself in a direction on along the bundle of sail. The diagram and photograph show this. Instead of tucking the working end *down* under itself it may just as well be tucked upwards. In both cases the effect is a chain of overhand knots spaced out along the sail.

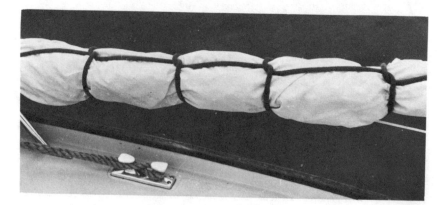

Waggoner's or Trucker's Hitch

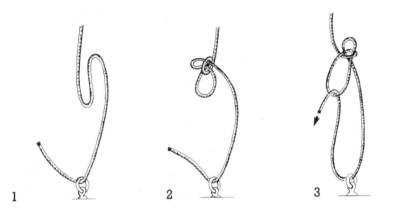

1   2   3

Widely used for lashing down loads on lorries, this Hitch gives a 2:1 purchase without the use of blocks or other devices. It's simple to form and falls apart when the strain is taken off it.

The line is first passed through a strong eye or under a securing hook. Two parallel bights are formed above the strong point, one upward and one downward. The upward one is applied to the standing part and twisted as though forming a Bowline so that the bight protrudes through a loop. The working end is then passed through the other (downward) bight and tension is applied to tighten the whole lashing.

Waggoner's Hitch in use.

Buntline Fisherman's Bend

This is an adaptation of a Fisherman's Bend particularly well suited to use with slippery synthetics.

The first round turn is as described for a Fisherman's Bend with the working end passing under the round turn. Then the working end is passed round the standing part and is used to form a Clove Hitch *towards* the anchor ring (or whatever) and is worked up tight.

Spar Hitch

This is something of a cross between a Clove Hitch and a Constrictor Knot. It grips better than a Clove Hitch where there is greater load on one side than the other, but is more easily undone than a Constrictor. To make the Spar Hitch a turn is taken around the spar with the working end crossing over the standing part before going round again. It then crosses over itself and tucks under the standing part. All that remains is to work the knot tight.

Sliding Figures of Eight

This simple bend provides the same services as a Carrick Bend in that it securely joins two lines of unequal thickness and remains easy to undo.

The working ends of each rope are laid side by side in opposite directions. Each is then used to form a Figure of Eight knot about the standing part of its sister rope, the latter being enclosed by one turn of the Figure of Eight (it doesn't matter which). These knots are worked tight and slid together. To undo the knot the bitter ends are simply pulled apart to slide the knots apart allowing them to be undone.

Stopper Knot

This is hardly a knot at all, relying essentially on friction rather than on binding. It is mostly used when relieving the load on one line by attaching another, such as when trying to undo a riding turn on a winch or sharing the load on a mooring cable.

A turn is taken with the relieving line's working end so that it crosses over itself (as in the first photograph). The end is then rolled on around the loaded cable for several turns before either being held by hand or half hitched to the cable. Load is then applied to the relieving line. The Stopper Knot can be undone even under load by releasing the bitter end and casting off the turns.

Bowline on the Bight

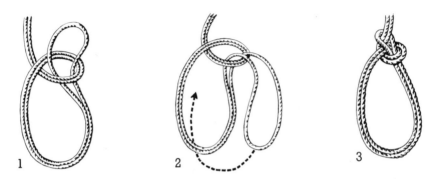

This is a good way of providing a loop in the middle of a line or for making an emergency bosun's chair. It's not comfortable to sit in but it does work.

To form a Bowline on the Bight take a bight of the line, apply it to the standing part and twist in the normal manner resulting in its sticking up through a turn of the standing part. The protruding 'ear' is pulled through, spread out and dropped over the two part main loop. It is brought up above the turn of the standing part and settled down. It then looks just like a doubled Bowline but without the usual end inside the main loop.

Spanish Bowline

1

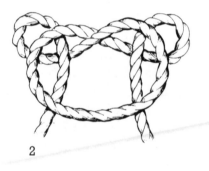

2

3

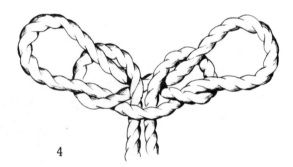

4

The Spanish Bowline, like the Bowline on the Bight, produces two loops enabling it to be used as a substitute bosun's chair or perhaps for slinging a ladder or plank over the side to form a paint staging.

Spanish Bowline's formation is unlike a true Bowline and is a bit complicated. Centre the rope and lay it out in three loops as in the first diagram. Fold the middle, large loop down, spread it out to enclose the two smaller loops and pull bights of the large loop up through each of the small ones, pulling them through as a pair of 'ears'. Settle the whole knot tightly.

Jury or Masthead Knot

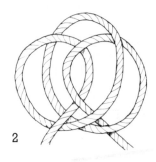

1

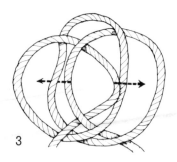

2

3

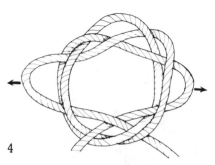

4

5

A Masthead Knot may be used for attaching shrouds to a jury mast or for erecting a temporary flag pole and many other similar applications.

Three loops are formed and interleaved so that the left part of the bottom one overlaps the right side of the top one in the centre of the middle loop. These two sides are then pulled out in a weaving pattern as shown and the top side of the middle loop is pulled upward. The process produces three loops and two tails, which can be linked to form another loop. The masthead or pole top inserts in the centre of the whole knot. Guys or shrouds are then attached to the knot's loops with Becket Bends.

Hunter's Bend

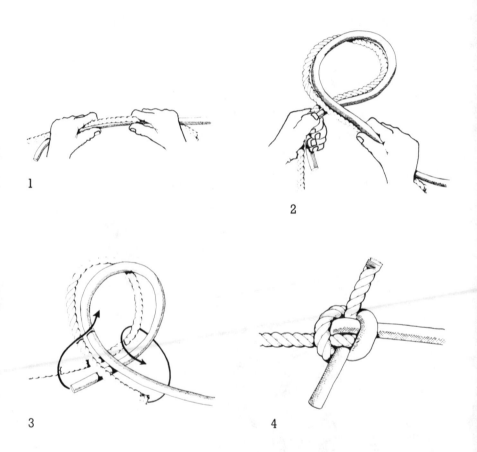

1

2

3

4

Used for joining two ropes together, the Hunter's Bend is well suited to stiff or slippery synthetic ropes. It is a square shaped knot formed by laying the two working ends parallel, but pointing in opposite directions, then forming them into a loop, and turning the working ends through the loop. The bend is then worked tight.

COILING HITCHES
Half Hitch Coil

Halyard falls should always be coiled up and tidied off the deck as quickly as possible; otherwise they become tangled up possibly causing serious trouble. The easiest and simplest way is to make a neat coil beginning at the cleat and working towards the bitter end. Always coil *with* the lay of the rope if it is a laid rope, as shown here. Once the line is coiled, hold it in the left hand, reach through the coils with your right hand and grasp the line near the cleat. Pull a bight back through the coils, twist it and slip it over the upper horn of the cleat, either directly or by passing it behind the standing part of the halyard for additional security.

Half Hitch
Coil for Stowage

A line that is to be coiled up and stowed away must be 'tied' in some way to stop it uncoiling. The quickest way is to coil the rope and then, using the bitter end, form a loop as shown, lead the end over the top of the coils and back underneath to emerge through the small loop. Pull up tight in a Half Hitch. The coil will remain secure if the bitter end is used to hang it on a hook in the locker or some other securing point so that the weight keeps tension on the Half Hitch.

Buntline
or Gasket Coil

More secure than the Half Hitch Coil, the Buntline Coil can either be hung up or simply laid down in a locker without coming undone. Coil up the rope in the usual manner but leave a long tail. Pass this working end round and round the coils (in an upward direction) to bind them together. Then push a bight through the top of the coils. Lift it up and spread it out so that it can drop down over the coils to lie at the top of the frapping turns. All is then worked tight and the fall may be used to hang the coil up. The Gasket Coil can also (as it was originally) be used to tidy up a fixed line in situ as shown in the photograph overleaf.

Buntline Coil used to tidy mainsheet.

2 Whippings

The basic purpose of whipping a rope's end is to prevent it fraying or unlaying, which is a waste; it also ensures that the rope will pass easily through blocks and eyes.

Common Whipping

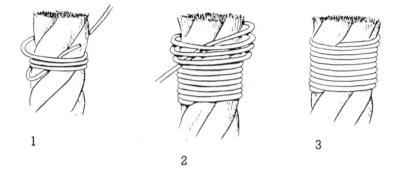

1

2

3

Not the securest of whippings, the Common is nevertheless adequate for most purposes. The basic method is to lay the end of the whipping twine along the rope (towards the rope's bitter end) and pass turns tightly over it to anchor it and cover it. Apply further turns, leaving the last few loose so that the end of the twine can be tucked back under them before they are worked tight to hold it in place. Cut off flush any excess of twine.

Alternatively, begin with a loop of twine laid along the rope. Apply turns over it as far as required and then pass the end of the twine through the loop, which is then drawn down into the centre of the whipping. Cut both ends off flush.

West Country Whipping

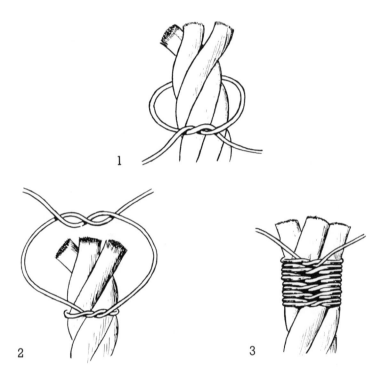

1

2

3

This is a more secure whipping than the straightforward Common Whipping but is a little slower to apply. Form a series of overhand knots on alternate sides of the rope; that is one at the front, next at the back, then at the front again and so on. When sufficient whipping has been applied, finish off with a Reef Knot (see page 2).

For further security in addition to using waxed whipping twine, give each overhand knot a second tuck (as for a Surgeon's Knot, page 27).

51

Needle and Palm Whipping

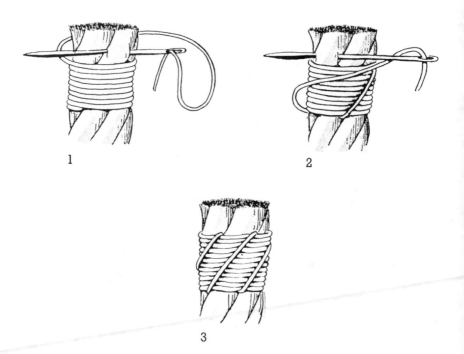

1

2

3

This is one of the most secure of the widely used whippings as it is actually sewn onto the rope with a needle and palm. Begin as though making a Common Whipping and, when sufficient turns have been put on, thread the twine through the eye of a needle. Stitch through one strand of the rope and worm the twine back down the lay of the rope over the whipping turns. Stitch through into the next groove and worm upwards. Stitch through again and worm down. Repeat, stitching and worming down until all have been doubled. Finish with several stitches through the rope.

Sailmaker's Whipping

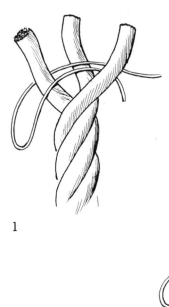

1

2

3

The Sailmaker's Whipping looks exactly like a needle and palm one but is not actually stitched to the rope, the worming parts passing behind each strand. To begin, a loop of whipping twine is passed round a strand of the unlaid rope's end, which is then laid up to include the twine. The rope's end is then whipped with the twine. The original loop is dropped over the end of the strand it was formed round and pulled tight using the end protruding beneath the whipping. This end is then wormed up to the top of the whipping and tied off to the other end of the twine with a Reef or Surgeon's Knot.

Alternatives to Whipping

A very quick, temporary measure to stop a rope's end fraying further is to bind it with adhesive tape. It is surprisingly effective but must be regarded solely as a stop gap measure.

A very tidy modern method of finishing an end is to fit a heat shrink plastic sleeve. These sleeves fit loosely over the rope's end until they are heated in a flame. The heat shrinks the plastic so that the sleeve grips tightly onto the rope.

Perhaps the commonest way to deal with a synthetic rope's end these days is to melt it in a flame so that the fibres seal together. A neat end is not all that easy to achieve as it must be moulded into shape without allowing it to stick to and burn your fingers. Try binding the end with paper, cutting through to neaten it and then putting it in a flame with the paper holding the strands together. Alternatively, melt the end, well wet your fingers and pinch it into shape. A hot knife blade may also be used.

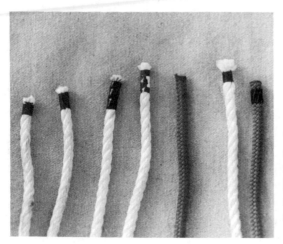

Types of Whipping (left to right): West Country, Common, Heat shrink sleeve, adhesive tape, heat sealing, sailmaker's, needle and palm.

3 Splicings

Short Splice

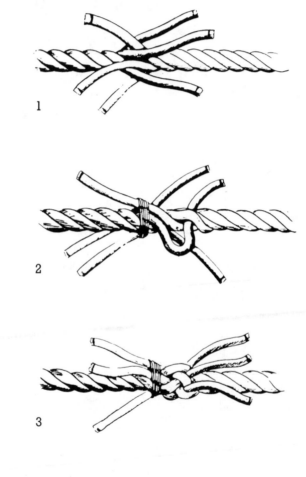

1

2

3

4

Several knots can be used for joining ropes together, but none is as strong as a Short Splice. It can cause problems by increasing the diameter of the line making it unlikely to render through blocks and where this is important a Long Splice must be used. To form a Short Splice the ends of each part to be joined are unlaid and the ends of each strand stopped with tape, or whipping twine – use a Constrictor Knot. The strands of each part are then married and one set of strands stopped to the other rope with tape (or Constrictor). The free strands are then alternately tucked against the lay into the other rope in an over and under pattern. The stopped strands are then freed and the same process is carried out on that side. After three or four tucks each side, cut off the excess of each strand leaving protruding ends. This allows the splice to settle without untucking. Roll splice underfoot to help settle it.

Long Splice

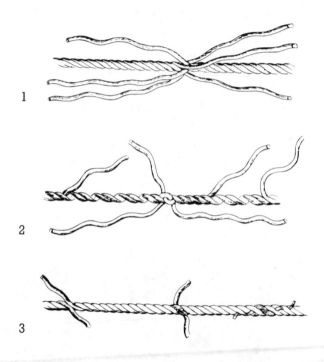

1

2

3

A Long Splice hardly increases a rope's diameter but is a little less strong than a Short Splice. It can be formed in many different ways, but this is a widely used method. Each line is unlaid for some distance (about ten turns) and the strands married. One strand each side is unlaid a further distance (about six turns) and its opposite number laid up in its place. Thus the line should always look like a complete piece of laid rope. Each of the three pairs of strands spread along the rope is now knotted to its neighbour with an overhand knot before being thinned with a sharp knife and tucked (over and under) against the lay of the rope. Again rolling underfoot will help to settle the splice.

Three Strand Eye Splice

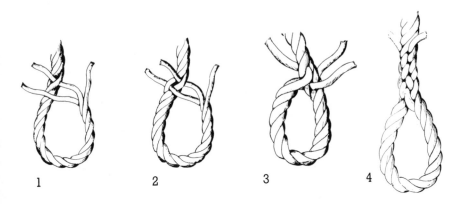

1 2 3 4

An Eye Splice provides the strongest and most permanent eye or loop in the end of a rope. Unlay the strands a short distance and seal or temporarily whip their ends. Tuck the middle strand under one strand of the standing part, against the rope's lay, at the point where you require the throat of the splice. The strand now lying on the inside of the eye is tucked into the next strand at the same point, followed by the third strand under the remaining strand at the back of the standing part. All tucks should be at the same point on the standing part. Next make three or four further tucks against the lay with each strand in turn. Cut off the ends; not too short, and preferably do not whip them unless appearance matters. Roll splice underfoot to settle.

Multiplait Eye Splice

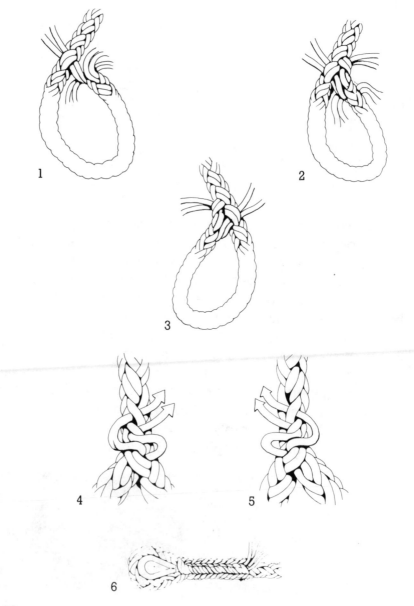

1

2

3

4

5

6

Multiplait rope comprises a plait of pairs of right- and left-hand strands. Right-hand strands have black marker thread. Form an eye to the right of the standing part, unplait and tuck a pair of right-handed strands under a convenient right-handed pair in the standing part. Tuck the adjacent left-handed pair under the adjacent left-handed pair in the standing part. Turn the splice over and repeat as above, using the remaining two pairs. Now separate the strands and tuck individually using the same sets of strands to give a characteristic 'parallel' appearance to the splice. Complete five tucks; finally, whip strands in pairs.

Stitch and Whip
Eye in Plaited Rope

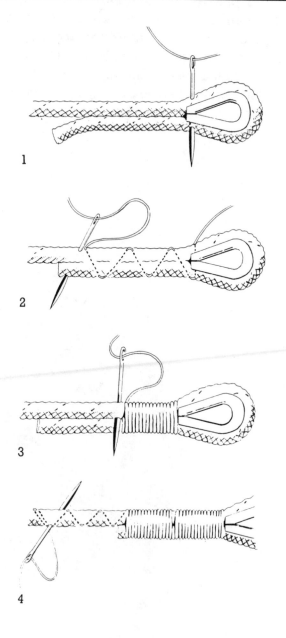

1

2

3

4

Not as strong as an Eye Splice, but plaited rope is almost impossible to splice, so it must suffice. Form an eye as required with at least 3 in (75 mm) tail measured from the throat. Using waxed twine stitch back and forth from the throat to the end and back. Cut the thread, and hammer the rope parts together. Now whip from the throat and hammer tight after a few turns. Halfway through whipping stitch through rope to lock the whipping. Continue to end and finish with several stitches through the standing part of the rope.

Marlow Sixteen-Plait Quick Eye Splice

This Eye Splice is quicker than the one originally devised by Marlow Ropes, but still requires careful concentration. Begin by forming the required size of eye. Measure one Marlow splicing needle length from eye and make mark A.

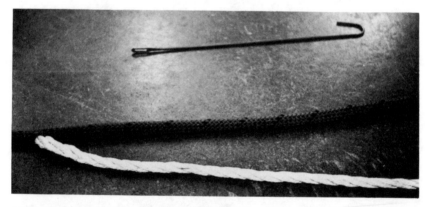

Carefully open sheath at A and pull out core

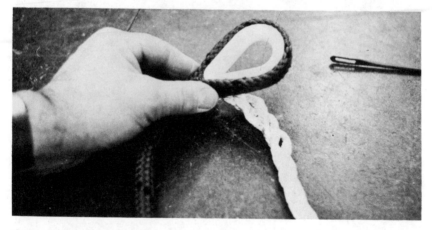

then form sheath into eye (round thimble) and mark B opposite A at throat.

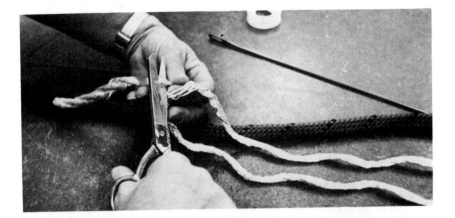

Tape core opposite mark B. Unlay to tape and taper
by cutting out half of each strand. Tape over ends.

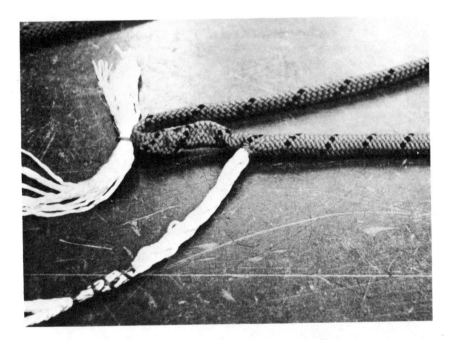

Insert needle along back of rope one length from A and
bring it out at B, concertinaing the sheath to do so. Thread
core and pull through to form eye.

Taper sheath by removing black thread to 1½ in below throat and cutting off followed by three more threads. Remove another four to quarter length of sheath.

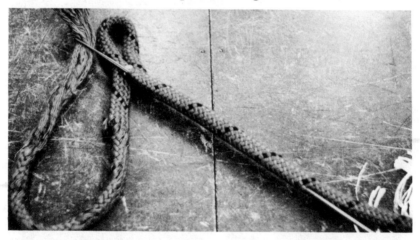

Insert needle on open throat side to emerge at throat.

Thread sheath and pull through.

Insert thimble and tighten, alternately pulling core and sheath tails.

Cut ends short and milk sheath to cover.

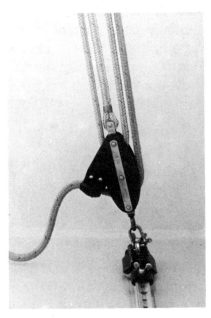

Braidline Eye Splice

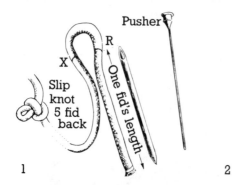

With its plaited core and sheath Braidline requires a unique form of eye splice. It needs a Marina Braidline splicing fid and pusher. Tape end of rope, measure back one fid length and mark (R). Form eye with R at throat and mark opposite point X. Make slipped thumb knot 5 fid lengths along rope.

Gently open sheath at X and pull out core completely. Tape end and slide sheath towards knot as far as possible before smoothing forwards again removing all slackness. Mark core where it emerges: Mark 1.

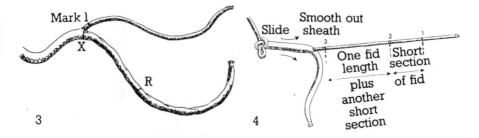

Slide sheath back and make Mark 2 on core one 'short fid length' (inscribed on fid) on from Mark 1. Place Mark 3 a further fid length + a short fid length on from Mark 2.

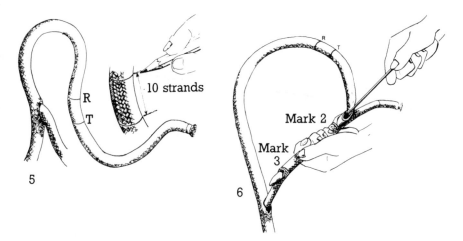

5

6

On sheath, from R count 10 strands (to either left or right) towards bitter end and mark T.

With 6 marks now made insert fid into core at Mark 2 to emerge at Mark 3. Using pusher ram end of sheath into fid and push through to exit at 3.

Pull through till T is at Mark 2. Insert fid into sheath at T, emerging at X.

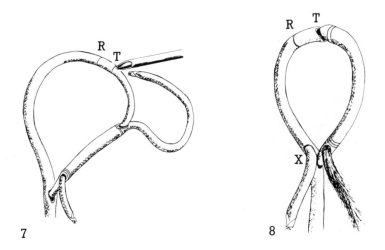

7

8

Push in end of core and pull through.

Hold core at 3, pull sheath tail to ruck core up against crossover point. Untape and unlay end of sheath. Cut away

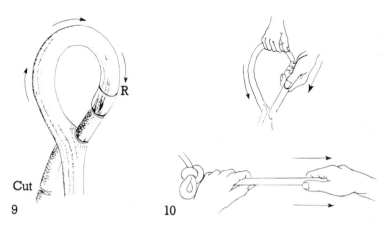

9   10

strands to taper. Bury by pulling on core at X then tapered sheath at 3 before holding crossover securely and smoothing towards throat on each side until tapered ends disappear.

Hitch thumb knot to secure point then milk towards splice (wear gloves against blistering). Mark 3 disappears, then 2, then T. Work to R pulling on core tail if necessary to clear bunching at crossover. Smooth round eye, cut core tail tucking last 1 in (25 mm) into throat.

Three Strand
to Wire Splice

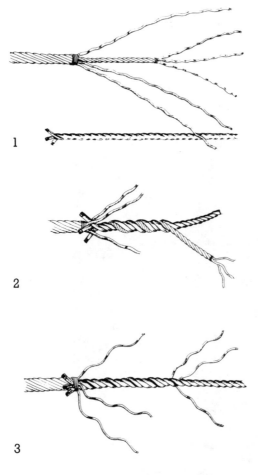

1

2

3

4

Wire halyards need rope falls for easy handling and if three strand rope is used, this is the splice for joining it to the wire. Unlay the wire about 30 diameters and remove heart if there is one. Whip wire where you stop unlaying it, also end of each strand. Lay three alternate strands up together for half their length and whip. Open end of polyester rope, marry strands with three long wires and seize together. Worm laid up wire right into rope then tuck both sets of wire strands against lay of rope. Cut off ends short and bury. Pare down ends of polyester and serve tightly over whole splice with twine or tape.

Marlow Sixteen-Plait to Wire Splice

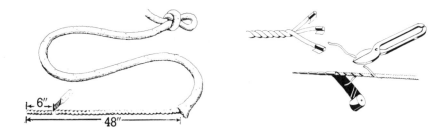

Using rope of diameter approximately twice that of the wire, make a slipped thumb knot 6 ft (1.8 m) from end and slide back sheath exposing 48 in (1.2 m) of laid core.

Cut 6 in off core and tape ends of remaining core strands individually. Taper last 9 in (225 mm) of wire by cutting out strands and then tape over point.

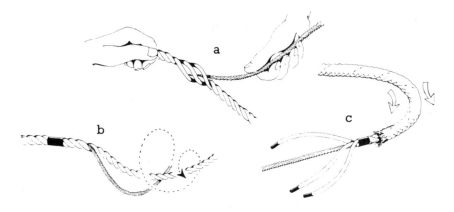

Insert this point into opened rope core 30 in (750 mm) from end, taping over to hold in place. Worm wire into lay until 8 in (200 mm) from end and tape over. Slide sheath over core to this point

then splice 3 strand core into wire against lay two strands at a time.

Make three full then two tapered tucks and trim short.

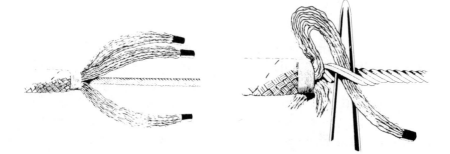

Slide sheath over splice and whip tightly. Unplait sheath and divide into three groups.

Tape ends and splice into wire *with* the lay, two wire strands at a time.

Neat spiral appearance should be achieved during five tucks, each one using reduced number of yarns to provide taper.

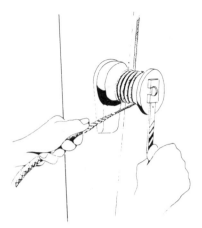

Finally cut off ends short.

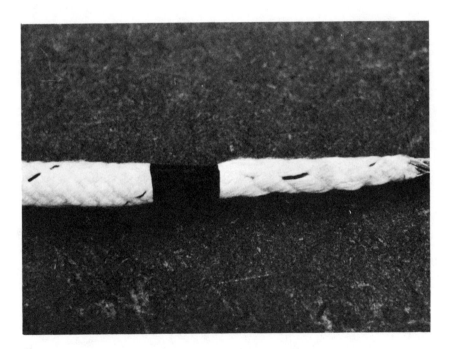

Braidline
to Wire Splice

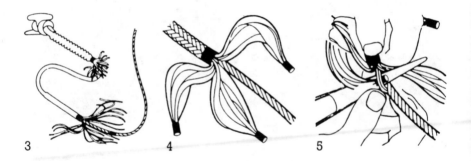

1
2

3
4
5

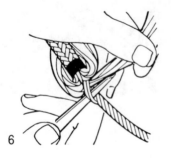
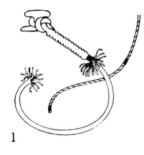
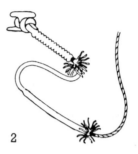

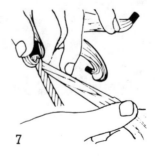

6
7

8

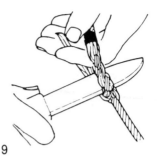

9

10

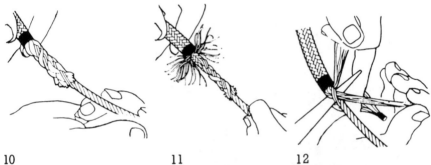

11

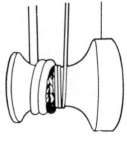

12

13

14

Make a slipped thumb knot about 2 m from the end of the Braidline and fix it to a secure point. Tape the end of the wire and put a tape marker 400 mm along it. Slide sheath back to reveal about 1 m of core. Slide full length of Marina Braidline splicing fid (obtainable from rope stockist) into

77

core from end and feed wire into it to tape marker. Gripping core and wire, pull fid out through core wall leaving wire inside. Tape core firmly to wire about 150 mm back from wire marker and unplait core to that point. Divide strands into three and tape ends then splice into wire against lay using two wire strands at a time. Make three tucks and cut off ends. 'Milk' sheath down over splice and tape tightly at bottom of splice. Unplait sheath, divide into three and tape ends. Splice into wire against lay for three tucks. Cut off ends and serve overall with tape.

Flemish
Wire Eye Splice

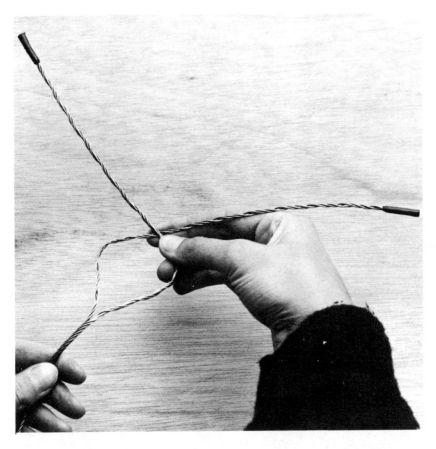

Suitable for wire *rope* (7×7 or 7×19) this way of making an eye requires no tucking and is therefore very easy, unlike most wire splicing.

Divide the rope's end into two parts; one of three strands, one of four including the straight core strand. Tape ends, then unlay to at least four times length of eye. Cross one part over other to form eye.

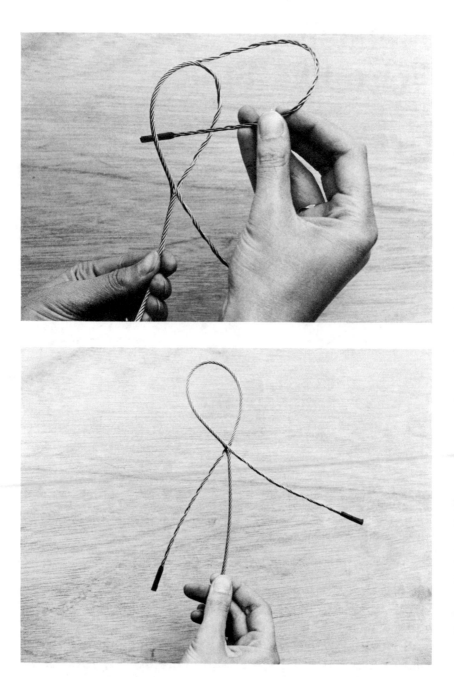

Take each part in turn and lay it into empty groove down opposite side of eye to throat.

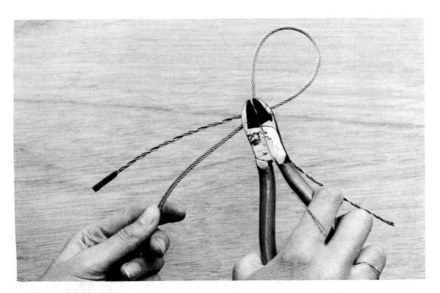

Cut out heart strand

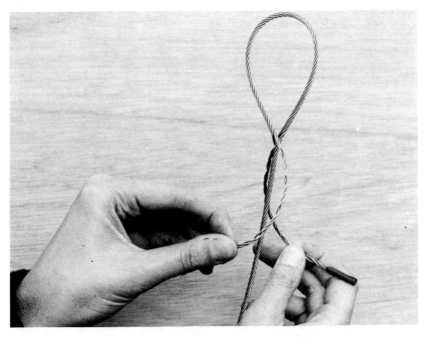

and, if required, insert thimble. Pull each part back to its own side

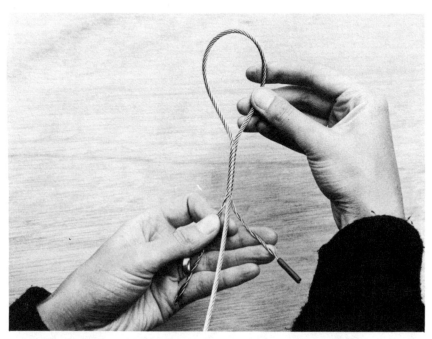

and lay up together spiralling round standing part.

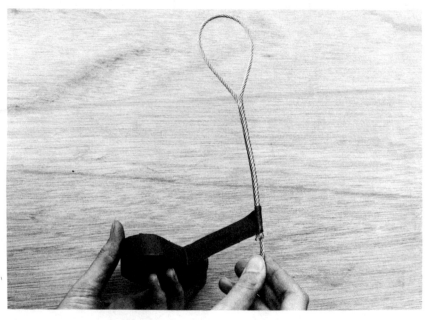

Serve over with tape.

Multiplait
to Chain Splice

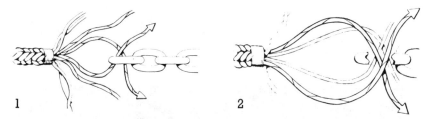

1

2

This splice allows a rope/chain junction to pass through a navel pipe or fairlead. Unlay four pairs of strands for a distance equal to 12 chain links, and seize. Look straight at the heart of the rope: of four pairs of strands one lies at the top, one at the bottom and two are crossed in the middle (see photo overleaf). Use the crossed pair for your first tuck. Either both have black marker thread or both plain. Separate strands in each pair and tuck through first link, two from above and two from below.

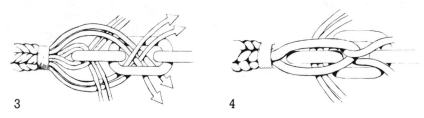

3

4

For second tuck lead strands along either side of first link and tuck crosswise through second link.

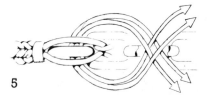

5

Pull tight to settle. Continue tucking with alternate pairs

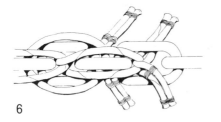

6

7

until 10 links used (five tucks with each pair). Finish by whipping ends across links.

Index